TALISMAN
FOR THE
SOUL

Andrew Bell

Talisman for the Soul

Published by The Conrad Press Ltd. in the United Kingdom 2024

Tel: +44(0)1227 472 874
www.theconradpress.com
info@theconradpress.com

ISBN 978-1-916966-05-5

Typesetting and Cover Design by: Charlotte Mouncey, www.bookstyle.co.uk

The Conrad Press logo was designed by Maria Priestley.

Printed and bound in Great Britain by Clays Ltd, Elcograf S.p.A.

For Ivy, with love

Acknowledgements

In writing these poems, I am indebted to many of the greats in the world of poetry, including T.S.Eliot, Philip Larkin, Mary Oliver, Pablo Naruda, and David Whyte; also to fellow poets Barrie and Ivy and all other writers and poets with whom I have worked.

Introduction

We live in a world of increasing disconnection, one where we appear to be separate from each other and at odds with the natural world, a world that is careering towards climate breakdown and ecological destruction.

I think poetry, with its sensitivity, and its ability to keep track of the constantly shifting nature of reality, is well placed to address the many problems that lie ahead. Although there are signs that something is stirring, there is still a long way to go. Poetry has to show that its voice deserves to be heard, if it is to become a vehicle for change.

The poems I write seem to grow by themselves in secret, often overnight, before something emerges. Whether they come as a single idea, or more usually, as part of a much longer process, one knows by experience that the poems have their own measure and their own will, and always take you by surprise.

It is like a bridging process, blending the inner and the outer worlds; always a reminder that poetry is not just words on a page that arrive by some logical process of thought. It is much more subtle.

Each poem seems to possess a life of its own, one that remains hidden, that holds on to its secrets, but is forever waiting to offer some insight into what was known, when the inner and the outer come together in everyday experience.

Much of my work is philosophical and meditative in nature. The poems seek to reconnect with the mystery and sacredness of human life by exploring the foundations of human identity through themes that touch us all: love and loss, humour, beauty, joy, relationships, and the natural world.

Drawing on my own life experiences, the collection explores this inner world with all its riches. These can speak to us, and teach us, in uniquely different ways, but more directly, and beyond the reach of that beguiling and bewildering marketplace of theories, opinions and beliefs.

Andrew Bell, January 2024

Contents

The poet needs to be up at night

when the world sleeps,

needs to be up at dawn

before the world wakes,

to live where others

don't care to look,

to show us the falseness

of our limitations,

the true extent of our kingdom.

Ben Okri.

THE INNER POET

Aspirations of a Young Poet

The way I would like to live,
the way I would like
to go on living,
is to tread lightly
on the earth, accept gladly
the role of steward,
dispel the belief
that we are somehow separate
from the world
and from each other;
share as much of myself
and what I have as I can
and do no harm.

hold fast to the dream
that we can live
peaceably together,
in a world
where beauty and harmony
may in time, displace all
that casts a shadow
over the human spirit;

in a community
where we may begin
to break down the barriers
that exist between us
discover the value
of cooperation,
as an antidote
to the stress of competition,
and see a shift away
from excess to sufficiency.

Where is the landing ground
for this vision? I don't know.
It will take time for it to sink
into the bones,
to see off those other voices
that would have things
remain as they are.

But I will keep on going,
keep on looking and listening
and taking note, keep on
talking to the earth,
keep on trying to understand,
until I'm ready to join
with others to find a voice
to speak it,
knowing that the wheel
is forever turning,
that the old ways
are now all but spent.

How to Read a Poem

I suggest you take a poem
and hold it to the light.
Then feel its presence,
as you do when you walk
into your first home
or into a holy place.

Does it have a pleasing shape?
Does its coach work
have any flaws or scratches?

Do the lines speak
to each other
in manageable slices?

Try walking inside it
and go into the rooms.
Let it speak to you.
Ask it to tell you its name.

Is the diction good?
Does it have a pleasing tone?
What about the choice
of words?
Would you be happy
if they were left within reach
of the children or displayed
in a public place?

Is it too wordy?
Watch out for this,
for in all your poems
you will find that less is more.

Now look beneath the surface.
Is it telling a story?
How is it coming over?
Do you need more time?

Are there any dark corners
that warrant further exploration?
Many poems are content
to be taken at face value.
They may be there to entertain you.

But you will find others
that carry layers of meaning,
calling you to unpeel them.

So what do you do?
Ask yourself: is the poem worth
further exploration?
You may decide to try again
and find there is nothing there
or be tempted to tie it
to a post to extract a confession.

Better then to pause and reflect
or failing that, to step outside,
take some fresh air
and go on your way.

Finding the Way to Go

How difficult it is
to discard the past
as it begins to capture
what will soon
become tomorrow.

How difficult it is
to kneel down
before the silence,
to drink
from the wellspring
of true happiness:
the holy waters,
forever there
waiting to break
the surface casing.

But now, walking
through the forest
on this crisp
winter morning,
I dip into this silence

and gaze upwards
as spangles of light
beam out
from the canopy.

Everywhere, the stillness
pins down the hoarfrost
dressing the undergrowth,
and is mirrored
by the stillness within,
as all thought subsides,
giving way to nothing
but the pure joy
of being alive.

Then later,
as the light within
begins to fade,
I watch
as those moments of joy
fall to earth,

arrested by words
rushing in to name
that which was known
in the silence
but without naming,
only moments before…

then watch as
they tumble into the past.

The way
I would like to go,
the way I have always
aspired to go,
is by the way of the poet.

No need to be clever
no need to judge
as an arbiter
of taste or belief,

I see the poet
as more like a witness
a servant of all that stands
in need of expression.

Never less than half a step
into self-forgetting,
is how I will find the path
that is always beckoning,
how I shall come to know
the way I have to go.

Keeping Afloat

This poem has lost its way
even as it tumbles
onto the page.

It's snaking through a back
catalogue of past hankerings,
the ones I have vowed
to cast off, but keep
bobbing up in various guises.

It's whisking thought winds
into shape and form,
making lines crackle
underfoot or fizz, as it tries
to be clever, setting up
sudden shifts of mood,
or conjuring a smile to break
out and land on the page.

This is part of the fun,
But poetry has many uses
and for some, it is more
a gentle movement
into silence,
a kind of freedom
of being here now,
of seeing things,
then coming to know them
before they become
ensnared by the past.

Sometimes, poetry evolves
into a kind of therapy,
as you enter into a dialogue
with your illusions,
learn to figure out why
you make the same mistakes,
or try to change things
that were better left unchanged.

Then it ripens into a kind of love
that calls what is seen and known
back to the surface
then just watches and waits
for the words
to fill with meaning
as they snap onto the tongue
or finger out from the hand.

It's a kind of love
that will tune into the poem
as it speaks,
listens to its benign inner voice
that will always tell you
when it's time to stop
and sweeps up the material
it no longer needs.

These things I shall never discard.
They keep the poetry afloat,
keep it going when the going is hard.

Taking Flight

Sometimes, numbed by the pull
of ordinary things:

the distraction of lists, dead
poems consigned to the bin,

the meddling of a restless mind
spooling through alternative plans,

the futility of keeping faith
in a tormented world,

I may talk myself into writing
a poem, then get seduced

by the urge to make it fly.
I'm already aware that this poem

is hungry, so I'm peering
into the sky, searching for clues,

asking why it throws no curveballs,
has no legs, no dash, no whimsy,

no singularity, feeds on nothing
but straight lines and shadows

careering out from sun-starved
clouds. But that doesn't matter.

Most poems do what they like.
All get what they deserve.

Poems like this one, having lost
their voice and fire,

with nothing more to say,
will just lie down quietly and expire.

Surrender to the Muse

Trying to write a poem freaks out my mind.
Working out a plan brings no release.
Yesterday I feared I might go blind.
I had to walk away to find some peace.

Today I'm wondering why I let it go;
got to reconnect, take up the fight.
Now I've got a line and feel the flow;
ordering my thoughts brought back my sight.

But then I'm thinking: have I got the time
to keep this up and find it's not much fun?
Should I stop and take to writing crime?
Or maybe pull the plug, just cut and run?

Well just as I'm about to blow a fuse,
a voice calls out 'Surrender to the Muse!'

The Muse speaks:

How sad it is to hear your tale of woe,
when all I have is here for you to find.
The thoughts, the words, the lines, let go
and so unlock the beauty of your mind.

The secret of this work is not to know;
to give up what you own and make a space;
then call up what you need and let it flow,
and so reveal the bounty of my grace.

Poetry itself speaks from the heart;
so build a pyre for your thoughts;
give up all claim,

just let the words come through:
make this your art; then give it all
away: turn loss to gain.

The words I here impart, will make you whole,
so poetry may speak directly from your soul.

The poet responds:

What does this mean?'

The Muse rejoins, playfully:

'Dappled pink
in morning sky,

webs of dew
in purple mist,

whispered tunes
in raging winds;

hear this dance
in endless space

and strains of Truth
in ancient springs;

breaking free is
what this means:

letting go
to find your wings.'

Thanks

In this new place
in the woods
I'm feeling the first hint
of the day's heat, surveying
the ground cover
for bark beetles and fungi
around the decaying logs
and stumps,

giving thanks for these few
special moments washed
by the wisdom of the earth,

and for the gift of learning
as the poet within strives
to cast a light
on the measure of things.

Then looking beyond,
I give thanks for those
with whom I have walked
and for the fearless
who come to themselves
when others hide
or refuse to do what is right.

and thanks too for the freedom
within, the place where I find
my soul lives, asking only
to watch and listen,
to find moments of quiet
for other voices to speak,

or moments that give permission
to offer a part of oneself
to something new.

It doesn't have to be a flash of
inspiration or a return
to a much-loved place or thing.

It could be no more
than a few words for a poem,
flowing from the hand unbidden

or just a resolve to do nothing,
to be nowhere else but here.

Unlocking Poems

Some words belong to each other.
Others have to be hunted, tamed

and harnessed to make them work.
Some need firing up to ignite others,

or careful watching to hear how they sing,
to see if they're good for a line or a piece.

In a poem, some people want something
quirky or funny,

but even more, they want things
that are hidden to be unlocked.

And the poet will try to oblige
by gazing upon the swell of images,

swirling behind the surface of things,
to bring something back for a dish;

or, by tapping into the secrets
from the further reaches, would pluck them

like hooked fish, to let them speak.
Others might look further still: by crossing

the threshold of voice and fire, into the holy
ground of silence, where gentle thought-winds

emerge and coalesce, they would whisk them
into shape and form, and land them on the page.

And some poets will just sit quietly and think,
letting the words flow through with the ink.

Then writing becomes a joy as they let it run,
chasing lines by colour, form, and scent,

watching leaves and flowers spring up
along each branching thought,

learning to listen, as the poem begins to speak,
making sure to set it free, when all that's done.

Writing

How difficult it is
to renounce the urge
to possess

to kneel down
before the ever-present
silence,
forever waiting
to break
the surface casing;

to watch the hand
holding the pen
and know
it is not you
who is doing the writing,

to trust
that everything
gets done
when the doing
takes flight,

when there's
nothing left
to stem the flow,

to know
when all is done,
for a few
precious moments,
there is only delight.

ENCOUNTERS
WITH MOTHER
NATURE

Doing Nothing

They say that life happens
when you're making other plans.

But today, there are no plans.
A storm has just passed

and I'm walking down the towpath.
After the rains, the canal is now a mirror.

Moving forward, I watch it copying
sequenced images of trees

dangling above; counterfeits masked
as holograms, piercing far into the deep,

quickened by their sharpened edges,
polished and pocketed in spangles

of light. And I'm taking stock,
opening up spaces beyond the tangle

of bickering thoughts, and the fancies
that write my existence; recapturing

those times I remember as a child
when, with no jumble of words

to hold me back, I might wander
down the lane, pick a stone and kick it

into the rough, doing nothing but watching
for the next one, or fix my gaze upon

the shadow ahead, as it tries to copy me
or find a few words to whistle out

to a shy robin somewhere above,
whose busy twittering might make

my tune feel it could go anywhere,
and I'd whistle to the sky.

Years later, someone told me we have
a soul. So I made enquiries and looked

into myself and said yes, but it dwells
in the silence. So I would begin to make

spaces, reel in those random thoughts,
and watch as others emerged to take form

and wing their way into the world.
And I began to see them all as part

of one family, where everything throbs
with a tune, each word as a note;

and how, when washed by the silence,
they could water the heart, or just float out

like moving spirits, carrying flashes
of inspiration, or words for a poem.

Pigeon

I was walking to the back door. She was sitting there.
A cold easterly was lifting the feathers

on a drooping wing. It seemed to be broken.
I squatted beside her on the edge of the terrace.

She didn't move… I watched, as any animosity
was quickly dispelled by a wave of compassion.

No clapping of wings, no cooing, no canoodling now.
Just a gentle composure, a quiet, almost matronly

integrity. I began to speak. To talk about winter;
the flooding that had lifted the drain, and the cold.

About being vulnerable; and how fearlessness will
sometimes intervene, when things go badly wrong.

She looked towards me. Then I knew that her world
was untouched by my kind of fear. And I spoke

of how fear was so often quickened by my kind
of thinking. And what it was like to be earthbound:

forever engaged in what was to come next.
And I wondered how it was with her;

whether she sensed that her end might be coming;
whether to intervene; whether it would be my hands,

that would hasten her ending, or something else.
With that serene dignity, she could have been a saint.

Motionless, she remained untouched by all notions
of loss or remorse, all those sentences implanted

in this higher language. Consoled by this thought,
I quietly moved away, as dusk gave way to night.

Loss

Why are we thinking more about loss?
For us, it was another night of wading
through the hard waters of grief.

I suggested we take steps to move on. I said
my mind would often stray into the world
beyond, witness remotely a far greater loss:
the weather's incoherence, places where fire
and water were fighting back. I would listen
to people on the streets pounding out
rhythms to stop the madness, or screaming
about some biblical payback for years
of self-defeating wars with nature.

But then, I would pull back, perhaps open
my notebook to find words to listen out
for nature's version.

'We are part of the earth and the earth
is part of us' said Chief Seattle in his letter
to the President in Washington.
'Every part of the earth: the shining water
that moves in the streams, every meadow,
every mist that moves in the dark woods,
every humming insect,
the perfumed flowers, and man,
all belong to the same family.

'What befalls the earth, befalls the sons
and daughters of the earth, for all things
are connected. The earth does not belong
to man. Man belongs to the earth.

Whatever man does, he does to himself.'

These words were written in 1852.
The Government responded by turning
their guns on the native tribes, and taking
away their land. And we were left
with stories about how the West was won.

I pondered on what this all meant,
what had been lost: the cost
of whitewashing the truth,
of pushing the earth for more
and more, of stripping out its soul
to appease a lightless world.

But I could go no further.

Though I do remember,
the following morning,
moving towards the door
before the darkness lifted,
then looking out to catch
an exquisite crescent moon,
pointing to a stately Venus
rising from the east, the two set
in a stunning cobalt canvas,
communing like twins, alone,
still holding on to the nascent morning sky.

Nothing else was left.
All words, all the loss,
and time itself, had gently passed away.

Source of Joy

Beyond the traffic
of the mundane,
beauty awaits,
offering itself
to those attuned
to its frequency,
creating a pathway
to the divine,

a bridge between
the two worlds
where time unites
with the timeless,

a confluence
framed by what
is perceived
in this moment:

the blackbird
perched high up
on a bare branch
of the sycamore,

closing the day
sweetly with its
full-throated song,

a line of native oaks
decking the horizon,
set against the rising sun
on a winter morning,
silent, unrobed:
a monochrome display,
all spidery and black,

the meadow,
with its flock of sheep
copied
by their long shadows.
cast in the vibrancy
of the autumn light,

the beauty, impressed
on the face
of a benign soul,
innocent of being watched,
radiant with light
and inner contentment.

This beauty,
this ambassador of love,
this pure source of joy,
feeds the human soul
offers itself
to the imagination,
washed
of all feelings of separation,

comes to us
as a simple presence,
the harvest
of a quiet mind
content to listen
and watch
through the lens
of the beauty within.

Snapshots of Summer

The May blossom, once laden
with exquisite snow-white sleeves,
is now long gone, but remains poised
in another world, to be reborn
in late summer, dressed
as the hawthorn's haws, ripening.

As the summer evenings wane,
and the morning light slips, the peonies,
once proud and brashly red, are now
collapsed with petals scattered.

The delicate rose, once feisty
is now drab and self-effacing,
and the tired leaves of the birch
and aspen appear patchy
and disfigured,
all slowly sickening, forever patient
in their readiness for the fall to come.

But always, there remain the pleasing
summer sights and sounds of childhood:

the insistent droning of a distant plane
breaking the silence
of sultry Sunday afternoons…

the stifling heat invading my upstairs
room, mitigated by the whining fan
my mother brought, bringing relief,
but interrupting sleep…

the persistent clicking
of the grasshoppers emerging
from the long grass behind the shed…

those long summer evenings,
when the day suddenly quietens
and there is a hush in the trees
as the sun vanishes below the horizon,
gilding the distant hills
with an incandescent glow
of ochre and red,
quickening the cloudless sky
to a delicious blue,
heralding a stunning starlit display
as dusk gives way to night.

And those rare and special moments
on hot and humid summer mornings
when I would rise early,
and looking out, would find nothing
there, but shafts of the rising sun
blazing through beads of purple mist;

and I'm left there, gazing out, bathed
in nature's arms, paying homage
to these little beings of light.

Crenelated Tower

However old you are,
you have been groomed
to be looked at.

If you are very old,
you may have had ropes
slung over you,
been hit by large objects
or seen humans cast
over your edges.

You may be a later edition,
a whimsical topping
to something below,
something more exciting.

But you will have gathered
moss and grime
and other accretions;
been carefully washed
or steam-cleaned,
because they know
you are the first thing
to be looked at, but only
for the length of a glance.

But if you're sitting
on a more luxurious pile
you are well set
to lose yourself
in the enchantment
of a much larger canvas.

Then you can expect a long
and happy life, can afford
to be self-effacing.

House Martins

Every April I look and listen
waiting for them to come.

And now, the martins
are here again, slicing the air

high above the rooftops
nimble and assured,

patterning the sky
with precision and grace;

and sometimes, as a pair,
darting towards the eaves

and lightly touching
as they survey the site

ready to begin the yearly task
of carrying life forward.

Fear would not occur to them
nor what might happen after

their work is over, and they gather
to make the long journey south.

Freedom is like living on the wing.
But here on earth we have lockdowns

with humans smarting at the loss
of things once taken for granted.

But we soldier on counting
our blessings, making coloured

stones or window displays
of rainbows, to remind us.

And, taking time to stop and reflect,
we step back into our communities

watch out for each other,
find new friends, share new skills

re-engage with the simple things
we knew we could always count on.

But now, as I watch those feisty flyers,
darting and wheeling above the trees,

and consider what drives them, peer
beyond their outer layers, I come back

to that which we share in common,
the place within us that just watches

all this, that is never constrained
and is forever free.

Rooks

Somewhere the rooks
have just risen from sleep,
peering down from the tops
of the sycamores and beeches.

I think of them now:
a silent army, paired, black-cloaked,
spooky in the half light, poised
to swoop onto the clammy earth.

There is only one question:
how to love this rawness of nature
in the unforgiving bleakness
of these dark February days.

I muse again upon these wily ambassadors
as they rise and fall on wedges of the wind
clever, industrious, assured, looking down
at man, aloof, unimpressed.

Whatever it is that defines this life:
the love, the poetry, the sacred earth,
places and things captured and held
in concrete and glass,

it is as much reflected in this rookish
intelligence, in its unmatched sense of family,
of habit and place; in its togetherness
and shared sense of purpose;

and beyond all this, the abiding recognition
of how long we have travelled with them,
and them with us;
how our lives will forever remain entangled.

Viper

I can be shy and timid.
I am like you.
I have my own territory,
protect my own space.
I am like you.

When I come of age
I might look for a partner
and dance a jig.
I am like you.

In the winter months
I pass time in our den
with my family.
I am like you.

I care for my friends
and sometimes
will shun strangers
I am like you.

When I am hungry
I may swallow my food whole.
I am not greedy.
It's just what I do.

This is how I am.
But this is also my pretence.
It is how I appear.
It is the viper in me.

Beyond this skin, I am you.
We are one, not two.
This is what I hold as true.

Speak to me proud man
Speak of what you know
Speak to me of what I am…
Say to me 'I am you'.

Swans

I have watched your lumbering
take-off, as you thrash and splash
along the silver surface of the lake;

watched you in full flight,
banking gracefully, then slicing
silently into the early morning light;

and watched you, in full sun, drifting
in the mirrored waters, making pleasing
crystal ripples fan towards the edges.

You do not need to look beyond
what is now, or engage
with what has passed, or hide like a root.

You only have to be what you are:
an emblem of beauty and grace, there
to ground us when we come to watch.

And for us, whoever we are, we may,
like the swans, let the world call us
to be witness to the rhythms

that nature has set, to find our place
in the larger family, where everything
belongs and nothing stands apart.

Bedtime Stories

You say you have heard bad
things about our troubled earth
and it's keeping you awake.
What can I do to allay your fears?

I could tell you another story,
perhaps remind you, now Spring
is here, of that secret kindling of ants
and beetles in the further reaches

of the garden, and all the liveliness
and merriment we found
around the lilacs and the birches.
Or tell you about that time

when a sparrow hawk thumped down
among the hellebores, ripping through
a collared dove, his fearsome eyes,
starlike, flaming gold, fixing me, boasting

his entitlement, as he spread a cloak
around his feast. I could have offered you
a sugar-coated version, but perhaps
I should trust that, in time, you will come

to know how nature really works.
Through the window, I can see the rain
beating against the pane.
You ask if we are in for another flood.

You want to know more: ask why
the sky is so often angry, why
across the world, they say the trees
are rasping for want of rain.

But there are some things I cannot tell you.
Questions about how humanity has abused
the earth: this shameful legacy
we have forged, that now seeks payment.

And, in me, the feelings of guilt: knowing
that I remain a co-conspirator, conniving
in this firestorm of complacency and denial,
looking on, even as the Gods of fire

and water are thrown out of kilter.
All these things you will come to know
when the time is right.
But it is late, and I must leave you to rest.

So let us finish with a prayer and remember
that in the end, it is only love that can heal
the earth. Then I must say goodnight, holding
a picture image of you slipping into sleep.

Dawn in the Paddock

I saw a veil being lifted
from my eyes, as the light
of the morning took hold
of the night, here
in this little sacred space.

Time now has passed away.
Gone too, the whirling fickle
frenzy of a mind intent on naming.

Now light plays with the webs of dew
and there's no desire to change it.

I'm dancing with the thistles
and the teasels, and chasing
splices of the rising sun that sear
through balls of purple mist.

Paying homage to these little beings
of light, in nature's arms
I'm lost in flight, to a world
in which all claim is gone,
where loss is gain and all is one.

FAMILY AND
OTHER
RELATIONSHIPS

Touch

As the air quivered with the first word,
flesh tingled with the first touch.

Through language and gesture, through lips
and limbs, as civilizations passed,

it kept coming… And by the lineage
of our lost mothers, it was reborn anew.

For this first touch is our inheritance,
the wavelength that connects us, the spark

that unites us with the angel of our belonging,
the channel that brings our soul light

to our brothers. But now, as shadows gather,
we see moves to change the order of things.

Touch, once tender, like a rose petal,
sublimely generous like its delicate fragrance,

is losing its loving presence.
Watered down by inhibition and fear

it has become detached from its language
of warmth and affinity.

Teachers, parents, lawmakers,
let us not unwittingly nudge it out of our lives,

lest we cripple the human spirit.
And let us not steal it away from the lives

of our children. Protect them, but do not disable
them. Let us not connive in this climate of fear

or demonize touch, sparking hysterical responses,
debasing it in legal process. Let our children know

that this is not the natural order of things.
Then let us weave this sacred thread into the fabric

of who they really are, through empathy
through the embrace or the caress, so that they

may, in turn, do the same for their children.
And may we remind ourselves

that it is not a shell that we inhabit. Living
and breathing through this tender covering

of skin, we are forever the ambassadors of touch,
forever ready to attest to its healing qualities;

to bear witness to its light, to become a channel
opening up to what was always there.

The Letter

I am well, thank you.
Sometimes I do not sleep
but at first light, may go
to those green spaces
by the river;
watch the city emerge,
watch for that train
that will bring you back.

We have been too long apart.
Do not let yourself be beaten
by all they have set you to do,
or let those thoughts
carry you away.
Be gentle with yourself.
Let go of that guilt
you feel about being idle.

I need to make a space too;
find things to take the strain,
until you are back here
and I can see that cheeky smile,
pepper hot and sharp.

You know we have so much
to smile about.

Do you remember that day I
told you I'd discovered
diamonds in your eyes

and later that night found
a cluster you said you kept
just for me, somewhere between
your thighs? And you blushed
but then you took me deeper;
told me of a path
that was always beckoning
calling us to wake
into another part of ourselves,
the part that is always lit,
that wants us to be nothing
but what we truly are, wants us
to live a life we could leave
alone to reveal itself.

Then that night, you said
you found diamonds
in the sky,
casting their light-shafts
into our darkness,
that earthbound darkness
you said we humans
had always thought
was light.

You told me that was the night
of your first encounter
with your soul light,
and with the silence,
the sanctuary
you had known as a child,
which had seemed to you then
like second sight.

Looking back, I can see
that these diamonds
we had so much fun with,
have somehow come
to define us.

There is much more of this
to be said, some other time.
Matter of the heart
can only go so far
between letter-writers.

My only thought just now
is to lighten your load,
so less from me is better,
for already, I can see
I'm making too many words.
I've been watching this
for a while now.
This may surprise you,
but it's something
I've started to work on.

I try where I can to hold
words to account,
to put them to proof in silence.

Did you know, I was once told
that everything is a word
like a sound, that carries
its unique quality.

So, more often now,
I will find simple joy
in watching and listening
to those countless words
embedded in nature,
and in the people I meet
in daily encounters.

Each word carries a meaning
that dwells beyond speech
and needs no words of mine
to make them real.

This is all quite new.
But even now, I can see
how much we lose by changing
whatever engages our attention,
in this constant urge
to define and possess.

There is much more to tell,
but that is more than enough
for now, my sweet... until next time.

Someone I may have known

He would never be found in a crowd
or be seen to jostle for position.

He doesn't do cleaning, washing
or lifting things. He leaves that to others.

They say he has a good choral voice,
though he would never admit it.

He doesn't write plays with actors
or plays about plays, or thrillers or crime.

He does like poetry and will write poems
about anything, even poems about poems.

He doesn't do hatred or aggression,
But if he did, he would keep it to himself.

He conducts life quite precisely
and can read people when he needs to.

He will tell you where they're heading
and to what end. He seems to possess

a sixth sense, and has said he works well
with mirrors, but only mirrors into the soul.

He will rarely get stressed or diverted
by unwanted facts, or allow doubt

to creep in. Curious about everything,
he would never rush to judgement

until he can see what is there. Age
and worry about time passing, would not

occur to him, for there is something
within him that will never grow old.

Who is this man? I should like to meet him.
I think I once did in a dream.

Beyond Appearance

It's a long time since I started probing
those dark inner spaces
and questions
like 'what is life and has it meaning?'

Well, not much has changed.
But now it's how these thoughts
might cross over, be put to use
in the life we have built together,

like how I might better handle
those occasions when you spoil
for another altercation,
or put my shoes in the wrong place.

Even now, when your father comes
and you give him our best room,
the one I have begun to use,
it's not a kindness, as it is to him,
but more a slight on this one
to whom your life was pledged.

But this poem isn't just about me.
Would you have put things in
I may have tactfully omitted
like the twists and turns in your life
with a man who, I now admit,
is racked by inhibition
and, as you would say, makes
procrastination his default position?

Well, not really. You would cling
to this veneer of propriety,
the web you seem to have spun,

giving the lie to all about the life
you have chosen, keeping it
out of sight, locked away
in those painful inner spaces;
and so would soldier on.

My game would be much the same.
I would pass over that messy catalogue
of awkward moments,
but would offer up instead, that painting
you did for me some time before,

the one with the neighbour's cheeky cat
resting on the back of our Afghan hound,
we still display on the wall by the door.

But giving place to what I now know
inside, I would add the redeeming
thought, that in your quieter moments,
you still return to those benign
inner spaces that lie just beyond
the reach of all my imperfections;

still aspire to rekindle the love
we knew from the start,

to hold on to what is really there,
putting aside all that we think we are,
but are not;

this, the more convincing reason why
we shall still soldier on, and never part.

Waking up on Earth

It's been a while since
this soul appeared
on earth, swept
into the darkness,
of a human vessel,
reluctant first to admit
to having arrived.

Now he's learning
to take words
like Lego pieces
from a box… learning
how to direct a small pair
of hands, to build
a platform for the life
he's already begun
to write.

The day of his
coming
and that fateful day
a cat jumped
onto his pram,
when his mother
was out of sight,
are beyond recall.

Now, as then, it's a life
lived from moment
to moment,
and here today,
it's Grandad
at rest in his chair,

his knotty hands
fastened
to his daily paper,
his voice solid
with kindness
and conviction,
and Mother
sitting close by…

two Gods
whose love carries
their every thought
he can still read
without a word
or a sound,

two Gods
who, one day,
will help him
make something
of life on earth
as he wakes
each morning
to his community
where people
find a place
to belong, a place
to love, to learn
and to have fun,

and to make
something of the
multi-layered
world beyond:

all-embracing,
bewildering
in its complexity,
where hearts
can harden and souls
become parched,
as inner turmoil
seeks resolution
in conflict and war…

two Gods who may
one day, remind him
that every drop
of blood,
every drop
of the rain that falls
embodies a blueprint
for the whole:

both the barren earth
and the holy ground
blessed with those
who toil to redeem
all that has been lost:
to move the human story
back towards the light,

to keep the way open
to the eternal presence
that forever beckons
that will remain with him
and will still be there
when the earth
and all the stars are gone.

Time to Go

He said his body had become as frail
as dead leaves, that it was now time
to stop for death.

He said he had taken time to reflect
and take stock, taken time
to throw away the accounts
he had kept with fear and regret.

He said he had never had a tryst
with God, but had come to feel
His presence every morning
if he knelt in prayer,
or just lay down and stopped the clock.

The people I don't know

I owe so much
to those I don't know…

I mean the ones I see
moving about, those

with whom I can feel
at ease, as I move about,

sharing their freedom,
knowing we owe

nothing to each other
and will never disagree;

feeling the peace
that comes with knowing

we can all love and forgive,
something I cannot deny.

When I follow them
or they follow me, perhaps

to form a queue, or listen
to some heavenly music,

or to gaze at a landscape,
things always go smoothly.

And I take comfort in knowing
we still manage to live

in three dimensions, keep
on top of those shifting horizons,

take delight in letting go
when the darkness comes,

knowing we all go on the same
single journey to the same end.

All this, a reminder of how much
is given, how much, in the course

of this life, I will have taken.
And I give thanks for all that.

Released

Sitting in the study, I'm watching
the early morning mist
give way to the rising sun,
waiting for your call,
waiting for the clock
to announce another day
captured by the call to work;

when I noticed a single stem
of freesia in a display
you'd carefully arranged, had split.

As I reached for the stem,
the delicate blend of purple and white
and the subtle fruity sweetness
took hold.

Time passed away, as the day ahead
took flight,
unlocking a few precious moments
here now ablaze in my hand,
opening up an inner landscape
where nothing is hidden
or set by the clock,
where everything is given…
Was this your call from another place?

where the love you have shown me,
has shown me how to love,

how that love may forever flow,
how it made me think and take stock.

School Photo Shot

Picture a boy perched on a bench,
in fifties vintage flannel shirt
and brown striped tie, smiling coyly
for the man crouching behind
his black blanket hood,
fixing a frame
through his concertina box.

And then the shot;
capturing a life
I had never before unlocked.

There's Miss Tranter wafting perfume
around my desk;
the rush to the school gates
to be embedded in my mother's dress.

Thirty years pass;
the man looks back, reflects…
Where is the link
between this simple soul
and this witness, now locked
in his striving for possession and control?

All I know, this is not the time to think
and take stock; but to find the peace
of this innocent world,
to find the joy of it,
knowing that what I have become,
that I am not.

Lost Causes

The head that loves
but only tenuously
that is found sleeping
when love thunders
or when the seas part.

The head that shifts
from one artifice to another
pursues lucidity in darkness

that feeds on fads
and all that's bad
and never seems to learn.

The head that spares
no thought for the things
that matter, like a flower
or small clouds
that glisten in the light,
or matters sublime.

I am that head
that has moved
between the two worlds,

the one
that makes the Gods weep,
preaching the language
of separation, the language
that has held captive
all earth travelers
since time began,

and the one
that has, at each interval,
seen this earth life dissolve,
seen it reach into the light,
come naked to its domain,
seen an end to the words,
seen loss freed from pain.

Our Ukraine
A message from Kyiv

So this is war: Crimea taken out
by unmarked Russian troops.
And now the main event:
shells hurling bodies,
still throbbing, through the air,
towns reduced
to mangled concrete and rust,
scorched flesh and body parts,
half covered in rubble;

the full horror played out daily
in emergency rooms:
rigid bodies with cracked voices
pining for help, eyes locked
in a stare which, one medic said,
was best unmet, even in a dream.

Yes, this is war: the rolling thunder
of Russian shells;
fire answering fire like chatter,
unspooling and spending itself,
then falling back into silence;
the perfume of relationships
put on hold, to be recaptured
as musings,
held close, like a balm,
to smooth over the pain and the fear...
the atrocities in Mariupol, Bucha
and Irpin, met with fierce denials
and disinformation.

No more war, said those leaders,
now long gone, before crushing
the tender spirit released
by the Orange uprisings, leaders
who taught us that corruption
was the only way to go,
setting up another round of greed
and hate, fated to come around
again, to face another reckoning.

Now, a new leader, honest, defiant
and media savvy, reaches out
to the world.

How will the world respond?
How will the history be written?
Will our voices be heard
when the story is finally told?

Or must we leave it to the politicians
and all those who were never there?

Why are we here?

Look at us. Fenced in by rooms
whose contents are now relics, legacies

of what we refused to leave behind;
numbed by words and idle thoughts

drifting between the many things unsaid
and ears that long ago stopped listening,

enfeebling what began so simply
with our first embrace.

Watch us playing God, building a temple
on comfort and whim, unmoved

by the stillness at dawn, or by a blossom,
or a flash of lightening on a distant hill;

a life stripped of untidy bits: things that leap
over furniture, or escape through the roof:

all those inconvenient encounters, that feel
like tests and trials sent to disturb the flow,

but come with stepping stones to a better life.
Look at us. What have we done?

Why are we here, sleeping? Come closer…
Listen! I have something to tell you.

Take the love letters down from the shelf.
Together, we can unpack the words,

the voices we once shared under the covers;
reimagine that lost symmetry.

We could still change the world, you and me.
We could be free of all this, if we try.

Let's do it before we die.

Words Within Worlds

We move into the upper gallery. Light pours in
from above, illuminating a screen attached to a wall

where we can see the whole drama unfolding.
Trying to piece together the story, an image

appears of an elderly man and a woman sitting
at a table on a terrace, deep in conversation.

We are in rural France, high above the Luberon valley.
It is early morning. Behind the couple stands their home,

a magnificent chateau, a place they have spent most
of their lives restoring, delivering, as both would say,

their daily supplement of joy. And a short distance away,
a substantial outbuilding, housing a vintage Citroen Sedan

kept by the man's father, but now slowly falling apart.
The woman is speaking. Does he have plans

to tend to this classic treasure, bring it back to life?
Any plans to start? There is a long silence… the question

had come before, but it now rumbles like thunder,
threatening to plunder what is left of his resources.

Casting a loving glance into her eyes,
he leaves the answer to find its way to his lips:

'Perhaps in another life', is all that comes.
Fortified by the silence between them, the words

fan out, take root in his mind, then roll into a dream,
to pass into the light when he died.

In the next gallery, a classic Lamborghini and he
its keeper. With leather upholstery and walnut dash,

there's nothing cheap, nothing brash.
Knowing he possess a stunning model, lovingly

restored, he bestows his attention with special care
tapping into its language on each encounter;

and with each word, each gentle adjustment of hands
and feet, it responds, cleansed of words that whine,

scream or screech, that cut in, rage, or drive thoughts
into tight corners.

For beneath this dazzling display of coachwork
and chrome, he feels a presence, a wavelength,

a soul life, releasing them both into a benign world
that feeds a feeling of having, at last, made up for time lost.

Old Flame

It came with a start, a cry,
from you, the bird flown free.
Step by step, catching your sound
from beyond the horizon
brought forth that call,
breaching the heavy pall of distance,
hooking itself to my antenna.

Together now, sifting palettes
of raw emotion, checking sinews
close to bursting, we speak out
the hours, trawling slowly-slowly,
touching memory's hand,
dew-lit on earthly delights,
spooling through what was once known.

God Speaks

You might call me God, come to ask me why
your sleeping world is in such pain, why the earth

shudders and erupts, why those merciless waves
rend the heart of your oceans.

I need to help you find the answers. But first
I have to ask you why you plunder the earth

pollute the air, the waters and soil, harden hearts,
bleed the souls of the innocent with your false gods,

preach the gospel of separation and blame,
why you abuse your brothers

with your corrupt social and political systems.
I need to ask you these questions, for I see you

naked behind the mask you have fashioned
for a thousand cameras, rolling about

in your shameless delinquency, startling the gods,
see you weaving toxic webs of deception

making chains, like perfumed flowers
on pretty, phantom faces.

The time will of course come when you
will discard this legacy and find redemption.

But first, you must enter the temple of humility,
release your grip on all this knowing.

Then I can teach you how to surrender, wean
you away from your false gods, allow you

to feel your way into the holy ground of silence.
And once there, I will show you how to reach out

to a new world of belonging where you come to see
that what you think you know is nothing.

And I will lead you to the delights of knowing nothing,
and from those hallowed grounds, teach you

how to move beyond, up into the realm of light,
to the end of all your suffering.

Taking Stock

The genial glow of summer has now passed
and I'm here alone.

The mist, now released from the valley,
hovers, mingling with a heavy sea fret,

washing the tree tops, its aftertaste
filtering through the open window.

Inside, the wall clock is sounding
its insistent tick-tock, tick-tock...

And I'm caught by the quiet spaces resting
between the beats; carried down the path

of silence, to that sweet spot that dwells
beyond the ordered sequence, where the day

is no longer calling to be filled or hooked up
to the clock, and the mind is uncaged.

And I'm posing questions, posting thought-lines
like missives, to the constellations,

reflecting on why you left all this behind,
straining to read the runes of your soul,

willing you to stop time, turn down the sound,
and speak your truth.

So today, I say, please do not call me again.
Please do not ask how I am.

Just ask why we cannot live here, as one,
ask what sweeps us into the forgetting,

and let us look beyond: ask why the reason for
our life on earth remains wholly undiscerned.

Then let me call upon the stars
and find an answer if I can.

THE FURTHER REACHES

Touching the Void

When I go, when I go down
into my thoughts
passing by the least articulate,

the ones I no longer strive towards,
and move on
to those that shaped me, the ones

that carried me to where I now belong;
and then, when I go beyond,
to the place where the past

falls away, where there is no more
taking hold or possessing,
only knowing... will you be there?

Will you be there with me as we touch
the threshold of thought and
the silence beyond, as we drink

from the still waters of the eternal
unmoving, catching glimpses
of our true inheritance, and will you

be there to bring what is hidden into light,
to watch the unspoken word emerge
from the void, to become the spoken word,

and when it is time to return, will you
go with me, and say what was known,
then shall we say it together in a poem?

What we do to God

Piously we circle around you
fashioning images that gather

in a thousand galleries, encircling
you with giant walls encased

in the deadening grip of ritual
or words of wrath that falsify

the holy books, uttered by those
deceived by their own fanaticism.

Many have gone this way, and may
have gone as far as the angels.

But still the Almighty remains
out of reach, until the walls tumble,

until the thinking ends, until time
gives way to the timeless

and there is a looking beyond:
a rising up to another realm

where there is only knowing,
where the One who would teach

can work with you in the silence,
in that holy place where you remember

who you really are, with nothing left
of your earthly sense - only joy.

Passing on

If I could reach
into the silence, to a still point

where memory and desire
are no longer stirring,

where loss is no longer loss
only a refining.

If I could say goodbye
to old habits, and old haunts,

all the unfinished poems,
and all those things

I have not seen or failed to see,
and hold no regrets...

And if I could look back
on all I have ever loved,

only to take away the essence,
and surrender all the rest,

then perhaps in the hour
of my passing

I could come to know the stranger
who is my soul,

and so return to the realm of light
where all are blessed,

having found release from the
ancient fear of death.

Being Human

Does the rain ever get angry,
or have regrets about falling?

Do storms get stressed when pressure
rises, or the sun waver before setting?

Does lightening ever plan its next attack,
or trees take from earth all they need,

then take more, out of greed? Do stars
ever change course, invading space held

by their sisters and brothers, then blame it
on others?

Do the Gods take time off before they die
or ever tell a lie, or forget the overall plan,

then go missing, as the earth shifts
and howls, and truth goes down the pan?

Is this all there is?
Or is there more to human souls?

Another voice that reaches out
beyond words and boulders of thought

to the holy ground of silence, a place
where all come to learn, and all needs

are met, where there's nothing hidden
and nothing wrong or right,

only something known by every human heart,
that all, in the end, must move towards the light.

Brahman

is never born,
has no need for blood
and bone;

yet its eternal presence
bodies forth as light,
like water from a spring

bringing shape and form
to all that may be known,
even to these words

as they listen to its voice
then swell out
and grow into a poem.

All voices, all words,
are like waves, vibrations rising
or falling, either redeeming

or ephemeral, like mind maps
mapping out illusions
then fading to nothing.

Often, I have felt the mind buckle
under the rubble
of picked over facts concocted

by polymaths, toiling to make
sense of the visible world
in endless columns of words,

unmoved by the silence:
by the wisdom of what can never
be counted or seen;

and others, building temples
of Babel, where holy books
are turned into weapons of war.

Starved of what lies beyond
they finally collapse
over cracked concrete and spoil.

And I have seen how personal
loss and disenchantment
can call time out, unlocking

the temple of the soul, replacing
fancies and distraction
with a lucid stillness,

as time unites with the timeless
to declare in the silence
the epiphany of becoming whole.

Going Back Home

The place
where no one
can lead you,

no one
can tell you
what to do
or where to go,

the sacred space
you brought
with you
when you were born
and have always known

the place
to which you return
when you need
to be alone

the place
where the chaos
and confusion
can fall away

as you come again
to hear the voice
of silence

come to be
what you really are

come to know
what it means to be free.

Having Been Born

After the reckoning,
and long overshadowing,

I am swept
into this other world
of shadows
and human struggle;

drawn to this earthed goddess,
sucked into the dark intensity
of her waiting vessel;

thence, from this abrupt translation,
into the softness of sleep.

She lies still,
there in her broken flesh,
in her ruptured wholeness,
torn by the burden of separation.

The light moves between us.
Still close to its source,
I can read her every thought.

And I want to tell her
what I know,
why I have come,
why we are one.

But I can only bring my light,
and bear witness,
until I too am swept
into the forgetting;

trusting that the time will come,
after accounts have been settled,
when I can tell her
what was once known

and we can unite in that knowing
and rejoice in it without words.

Holding Fast

A long time has passed
since that moment

when you finally knew
what you had to do,

and began.
Even as the voices

around you, kept on pulling,
chasing past delusions,

you kept on going,
curious, emboldened,

led now by a new voice:
your soul guide,

come to light up
each successive step,

to keep you on track
as you moved deeper

and deeper into the world
of form;

knowing that if you ever
took your eyes off the goal,

or closed down your heart;
ever set out to harm

or settled for less
than the good and the true,

you would have stepped
off the path forever.

Letting Go

He said he had become tired
of watching time pass
tired of moving about
in his own shadow
like a ghost from the past

tired of being consumed
by every creeping thought:
bits of plastic and rubble
contaminating his inner
landscape; summing up
a shadow life kept carefully
wrapped and out of sight.

Now he's taken to gazing
at the clouds
watching them
speak their language
to empty space:

puffing balls of cotton gently
changing shape, keeping pace
with the dance of light
then thinning to nothing.

And he's wondering
whether to follow their cue
find some way
to let go of the past

but then worrying
what it would be like
to end up with nothing.

Then he remembered
what he was once told,
that nothing
is just an empty space
like a place to rent,
where all things unfold
only to return
once their lease is spent.

So he begins to watch
each moment, as each new
rising thought advances
to its peak
then moves into retreat,
yielding up its voice
to the one that follows,

then watches
the whole process repeat,
watches as the past
keeps on falling.

But now he's asking where
it's all going,
still looking for some means
to lighten the load.

The answer comes through
in one consoling thought:

there is always a moment
when time loses its beat
when the present is lit
when the mind
breaks loose from its spin…

always a place on earth
where thoughts can venture out
and make friends with each other
or commune together
in a flush of tiny bubbles
of laughter and mirth.

Morning

A late awakening
it was this morning;
caught up
in the mind-net
I call my private world.

Lost, but willing
once again
to surrender,

to hitch a light-shaft
to the edge
of all this knowing,

to fall
into the holy ground
where nothing begins
and nothing ends;
where the constellations
play through the life
and all is praise.

Rapping Home
(after Kate Tempest)

I've been looking at humanity
drowning in its vanity
trying to make a future
from diminishing capacity
sapping its vitality.

See it, take it, then come back
for more, give it to the rich,
leaving nothing for the poor.
Yes, we've heard it all before.

But the stakes are all changing
the planet's now expiring
and we're still waging war.

So what can you do when nothing
goes to plan?
When there's falsehood
and deception
and truth goes down the pan?

Is there anybody there
to give succour to humanity
bring back some sanity…

the ones who make things happen
the beneficent and wise
or those who speak in riddles,
the ones who tell the lies,
who make anger and abuse
a legitimate excuse?

There are some of us who'll swear
there's a God out there in hiding,
a God who rules the world.

But for others, that's just a fiction:
He's either lost all conviction
or He's not really there.

For the Gods are all around us
still trying to tell their story.
You can see them in the High street
checking Twitter on their phones
you'll find them in the pub
and meet them at the races
in office blocks
in betting shops,

and, in various open spaces,
there are others seeking meaning
in passionate embraces.

They say these Gods are all
within us, trying to tell the truth.
Well for some, that's too abstruse,
it's not their mission,
not their tradition,
just a useless proposition.

So who are the heroes
and who are the villains?
Well now I'm all confused!

Should I refer this to divinity
re-establish some affinity,
some connection with a deity
perhaps invoke the Holy Trinity?

But my head is really spinning.
Is there something more fulfilling
like a God a God could trust
or clear-cut definitions
of what's rational and just?

So I'm speaking to the silence
and asking simple questions…

Is it okay to ask for guidance?
okay to admit defeat
by leaving poems incomplete
or poems lacking clarity?

But I'm wandering off the point
I must ask with all sincerity,
is there a message for humanity?

Is there anybody listening?

Is there anybody there?

But there's nothing coming through
not a word, nothing more
than the simple recognition
that the truth is very simple,

that there's really no damnation,
no retribution,
no hell, no death, no devil,
no God in the sky, no separation;

only a love that asks for nothing
that assumes no positions,
a love that loves without conditions.

Return to the lost Planet

First time out, we arrived on a shaft of light;
falling into your troubled world, weeping tears of gold.

Cast into the Underworld, we saw how Lucifer
and his legions had infested the Earth.

Saved from a plague of serpents, we witnessed
the heavenly hosts do battle with the forces of darkness.

Then we slept for a thousand years; were watched over
and tested, before the Lord of the Earth made us his own.

And we were taken to Noah to direct his people
in the construction of an ark,

made from a deserted palace requisitioned by God.
We heard the sacred dialogue between the Lord Krishna

and Arjuna before the battle of Kurukshetra,
gave comfort to the Son of God at Golgotha,

watched over the cave at Hira, as the Qur'an
was dictated to Mohammad by the Lord of hosts.

And we laboured together through many lives, working
with the forces of light, to counter the forces of darkness,

enduring hunger and suffering as warriors and slaves.
We taught you many things and were distraught

when you did not hear us, or took no heed of our warnings.
We knew that was the way of the world; that we were never

sent to persuade or cajole, only to lighten the load.
But it was when your Earth started to burn and to flood,

when we heard your collective cries for relief from the chaos
and the pain, that we knew it was time to make our final pitch.

Working with your best people, we helped you move
towards a solution; to find a new way forward.

And you came to see that you were not separate
from your Earth Mother and not separate from each other;

that you could put aside the selfishness and greed
and work together for the common good.

We knew then that our work was done, that we too
had found redemption; that we could now return to our home.

Say What You Mean 1

That moment you
came to know
how things are said
but not felt,
passed to others
but not understood,

came to know
how language
can become a pretence
like a hollow reed
hiding an imposter.

Then that moment
you resolved
to move beyond,
to the frontier
between speech
and silence,

tapping into a place
blessed
with nothing more
than spontaneity,
the child of what
is only ever now,

the place where
you could listen
and hold back until
there was something
to say, something
that would find words
to say what you mean.

Say What You Mean 2

In the moonlight,
in the early hours,
I step out
into the lane, a presence
enveloped in the silence,
becoming a shadow,
cast by a line of oaks
black against
a clear indigo sky.

A gentle wind
is ghosting
through the trees,
permeating
this shadow life
like a winged gift,

clearing a space within,
teaching me
that what is real
is forever
what is happening now,

that our true voice
may be heard
when we give time
to the inner life,
when the inner
and the outer
become blended as one,

and when,
in those few moments,
the voice can speak,

as we let the words
come through untracked,
like sweet calling cards,

catching them
in that unique conjunction
before they are gone.

Soul Searching

The head that loves
but only tenuously,
that is found sleeping
when love thunders
or when the seas part.

The head that shifts
from one artifice
to another,
pursues lucidity
in darkness,

that feeds on fads
and all that's bad
and never seems to learn.

The head that spares
no thought for things
that matter,
like the flowers
or small clouds
that glisten in the light,
or matters sublime…

I am that head that has made
the Gods weep,
preaching the language
of separation,
the language that has held
captive all earth travelers
since time began.

And I am that head
that has, at each interval
seen this earth life dissolve,
has reached into the light,
come naked to its domain,

seen an end to the words,
seen loss freed from pain.

Dialling Down

Tread lightly in silent places,
heart open to brief encounters
find rest in unwatched spaces.

A light rustling
in the whitening willow
will retain its beauty
if we pause to meet it,
may thin to nothing
if we strive to seek it.

Turn off the engine, quell the
babble of all that's running:
the mulling, musing,
the notes left playing.

A true voice builds its kingdom
in the soul,
dwells in silence,
makes all things whole.

The Word

What are these words for?

His mouth was full of water and words,
lines, like bits of paper

careering out from a world of fancy,
trade waste, betraying an unholy past.

He asked of others if there was something
more, something beyond these voices.

They left him with a raft of choices
but he was soon lost again in the lines.

So he turned to himself and asked for a reply,
for a way out of this shaking world.

And he moved to another country where they
taught him how to dwell in the silence.

And there came a moment when, with a single
focusing, he let go of all his knowings.

Then he watched the thoughts and words
blend together in a lucid beauty like scented

flowers, his best lines flowering forth
from the stillness, seductive like the summer

hollyhocks, standing proudly above the mass.
And he was taken to a holy place

where they told him of the sacred song above
the earth, of the first Word and all its progeny.

And he heard the silence speak
from a place where there is no speech.

And with nothing left to hold him back
he raised a cup to the life to come, to the silence,

and to the Word, the pure wine of language,
and drank from the words that water the heart.

Transformation

It could be a mistake
to believe
in an immortal soul
but to carry on living the dream.

Already something calls you
to make a choice:
is it that emissary
of the Gods that dwells
in your presence unseen,
holding the silence
when you speak,

or the dweller on the threshold
of a world where death
takes everything away
and nothing comes to rest?

Even now, there are glimmers
of the light within,
stirring slowly,
gently tapping into your life.

View from the Window

Each bitter February day eats
a little further into the bone.

But today, all is calm, with time
and space now bound together

in silence. Through the window,
the first light is rising, casting

a rosy hue over a clear cobalt sky.
Beyond the houses, the sycamores

and oaks stand in line, stock still:
spidery and black, they deck

the skyline: a monochrome display
sharpened against the nascent light.

Below, in the street, still untouched
by the rush to begin,

there's nothing to break the silence.
No children in the school yard

doing what children do, no heavy
thrum of engines, no putrid air thick

with the stench of hydrocarbons,
only a lonely plane passing overhead,

its silver underbelly pushing back
the dawning light. And here, a mind

at rest, eyes locked on this blazing
pageant. No more harvesting of words,

no thoughts unhinged; just a letting go,
a feeling that this is what it's like to be free.

What I Am

What I see
I am not,
what I hear
I am not,
what I know
I am not

What I am
I see not,
what I am
I hear not;
what I am
I know not.

I am that
which stands
behind
this one
that thinks,
holds
the silence
when he speaks,
watches
when he moves.

The One
that carries
the flame
when he dies.

What I Have Come to Know

We who breed
and consume,
forever marking out
what is ours,
rarely reach down
to where the meanings are.

But when I'm out in the woods
perhaps wandering
in the undergrowth,
waiting for something shy
to come frisking out
from the leaf shade,
or watching a cheeky robin
sounding out
its convoluted song
- was it a welcome
or a warning?
I could never tell;

then sometimes
a stillness descends
as the landscape listens,
carrying me
into the calm
of the landscape within;

and watching there, I see
how a mind unhinged
can distract,
how much is lost,
how the beauty
of our native wildness

is blunted,
how an unwatched mind
reins in
those great shouts of joy,
forever waiting to be born.

But then, when the soul stirs,
see how a single sheet of light
can whisk away
whole catalogues
of intrusive thought.

I remember once when
when out in the woods,
finding the robin
hiding in an ancient oak,
and knowing then
that his song *was* his truth,
knowing how nature
never fails to carry
what is hidden, into light.

As we humans
speak our truth
what if we followed
nature's law, but willing
to hold back the words
until they are palatable,
or pleasing,
or made ready
as an offering,
to flower forth like roses
giving off their scent?

And what if we were to listen
to the spirit seeded
in another world, happy
to welcome it into this world
willing to listen
to its message,
to let it offer its light,

happy to know
that we are that light,
that the light is what we are.

Freewheeling

I stand
before the clear waters
of the eternal unmoving,
locked
in my little god-pack,

still playing God
but watching,
straining to loosen
the claims
that I call thinking

to drink from
from the still waters,
thence to fly,
to rise up
into the world
of names and forms

and then, with all undone
to let it be.

HAVING
FUN

Terminal 9

Your attention please!

Flight No. 29, The Errant Wind, bound for Missing Springs, is now boarding. All passengers please proceed to the Gate marked 'Sleeping'.

Your attention please!

Flight No. 32, flaming red and raging, is now departing from Gate No. 3, bound for patience and contrition. All passengers may now begin boarding, providing further noise is muted.

Your attention please!

Flight No. 64, the Cyber World, is no longer in service. Tainted by deception and double-dealing, it has been grounded by Security, and is undertaking restitution.

Your attention please!

Reports are coming in that the old order is now crumbling, that the Gods are returning to earth, and a rescue mission is now beginning. They are telling us that the human soul, for so long silenced, is now stirring, and there will be much rejoicing.

We can therefore announce that all passengers are free to dance a jig, or may proceed to the Heavenly Gate, to move beyond this earthly arena.

Finally, we have been asked to reassure you
that you will encounter no more gates or barriers, no more checks
or double booking, and no more forced detentions.

There will be more silence, where you will find love,
where you will draw closer to each other, as you rediscover
your lost lineage of joy.

So please take your place with all those who have left
their place of hiding, and before you depart, please bestow
blessings on all earthbound souls remaining.

And be assured, there is no further need for directions,
and nothing more to do.

Just step outside, and the Gods will be there to greet you.

Mr. Verity

A friendly stranger has taken over
the top floor in my head.

A man of culture and refinement,
he wears smart shoes,
with polish well rubbed in;
keeps his best thoughts
in his wardrobe on the shelf
above his suits and ties
and his aspirations,
in other fine pieces,
some suitably distressed.

You will never hear him grumble
about errant thoughts leaking
through distressed tap washers,
embarrassing moments,
or missed opportunities.

But I suspect he has come to teach me,
hold a mirror to my foibles,
or because he never seems to rest,
reset my synapses as I sleep.

More often though, I will find him
playfully disrupting my self-absorption,
like when he sings melodious refrains
through the floorboards above my bed.

At weekends, I may accompany him
in duets, and sometimes,
when I miss a beat,
I can see by his look,

that I'm somewhere else,
reliving those Sunday afternoons
with the lady I met in the flat below,
the one who keeps my dreams
with her rings in a box.

And when the world is having fits
about this or that,
or when I get caught up

with the problems of mortality
or the properties of dark matter,
or eternity,
or I'm wondering whether writing
a poem is a symptom of insecurity,

he answers my questions
with thoughtfulness and grace.

Then my attic voice begins
to change its tone.
I'll feed on benign spaces between words,
put the issues back in their chest,
slip quietly into those silent attic spaces,
and make a cup of tea.

Election Fever

It's half past nine on a Sunday morning.

Sitting on the steps beneath
The Old Market Cross, I'm waiting for you.

Little platoons of cars advance onto The Pay
and Display, squatting on the bleached tarmac

that was once a busy market square.
A jet2.com flight from nearby Robin Hood

creeps silently over the Crown Hotel.
The smell of fetid fungi escapes

over the fields from the mushroom farm,
mingling with a heady cocktail of diesel

and coffee beans, as it hits the neat columns
of coachwork and chrome, now dressing

the square. I'm accosted by a man
with a pony tail, clutching a big furry creature

dangling from a pole above my head.
He wants me to speak to it.

But I'm somewhere else. This is not my business.
Today, it's the Town House Coffee Shop with you.

I look up thinking I might tell him
I don't do elections on a Sunday morning;

but the furry creature is already moving off
and I'm left gazing into the space

above the trees, following a sleek silvery dart
slicing silently into the morning sun.

But turning into the street, another one
appears. It looks like a big brown bear,

but it speaks like a woman disguised as a bear.
It's now invading my space and scratching

my head, telling me it's the official candidate
for the Big Brown Bear-hugging party

and it's looking for support. And before I know it
I'm into this monster hug, and it's licking

my ears, and I'm thinking: 'this is a good one',
but I need to get my face out of its neck…

I need to think about the issues.
But I can't. This is not my business.

Today, it's the Town House Coffee Shop
with you. But I'm already on a high

and I'm thinking maybe I should try a hug too.
And I'm looking at strangers

and wondering whether they might like one.
But just as I'm reining myself in,

you appear by my side.
Hold on tight I said, this one's for you!

Imagine

What if the world
went into lockdown
and all phones were muted,
pushing humans awkwardly
into a covenant with silence?

Or the light of the sun filled
the light in our heads,
unmasking all thoughts?

What if the constellations
sent emissaries of light
to earthbound souls, with messages
more precious than gold?

Or ancient oaks began to speak,
unlocking the secrets of the past?

What if you took a picture of a tree
and the leaves began to shimmer,
then later, a bird appeared
to sing you to sleep?

Or a phoenix and a dove appeared
at your door and became your mentors?

What if the earth, for so long unloved,
upon which we have walked blindfold,
still held us,
still offering everything we lack,
and we finally gave thanks?

or our teachers could,
with a single wave,
erase the relentless pressure
to achieve,
to quell the raw, silent scream
of anxiety and fear.

And what if all these things,
opened a few precious moments
to think and take stock,

to rebuild this earth temple,
to capture the vision
of freedom, justice and peace?

Ode to the Door Key

Every morning you take me
from the hook,
rush me into some grubby pocket
or mildly fragranced handbag
then pull me out, so I can perform
naked in the same dark hole.

Then the whole trauma
of withdrawal:
an unceremonious wrenching
at its worst;
but when you put attention
first, a gentle disconnection.

There are no rest days
in this engagement
but comfort breaks at every turn,
making up
for any inconsiderate handling.

Occasionally I get entombed,
starved of light in the lining
of some forgotten pocket
cast aside for a season
or laid to rest
between your car seat
and the door, just out of sight.

But today, an unexpected pleasure,
something not to miss:
you're apparently off to Paris
having taken the other key:
the nearest I'll ever get to bliss!

Smart

You're smart because your dad was smart.

I'm simple because my Mum and Dad
led simple lives.

You're smart because you can think
on your feet, and make speeches
without notes.

I'm simple because I don't think like you
and don't make speeches.

You're smart because you think
your Queen's English is a passport to success.

I'm simple because I don't know what success
is, but mainly because I have a verbal tic
which annoys you.

You're smart because you don't bother
to compete, but know how to win.

I'm simple because I don't try to win
and don't know what it means to compete.

You're smart because you never say yes
without an escape clause.

I'm simple because I like to call a spade
a spade, and keep three in the shed.

You're smart because you would never
admit to eating chocolate, even between
consenting adults.

I'm simple because I do like chocolate
but give most of it to the food bank.

You're smart because you spend
all your spare time in your Bugatti
and get your nephew to repair it for free.

I'm simple because I'll spend hours fixing
the brakes on my Austin 7 and years
sourcing second-hand spares.

But what if all this is just a game?

I could have said that you're simple
because you think you know everything,
when it's really just a pretence,

and I'm smart
because I can see what you're up to.

But I'm peering behind the words,
behind the labels and naming of parts,
to a place where nothing is hidden,
where ideas can make friends with each other,

a place where I might just laugh at myself
or happily admit to knowing nothing.

Haiku

They said: 'Peace on Earth'
for an age, in words and song,
and still got it wrong.

———

There's always a point where words
slip, trip off the tongue for the wrong
reason.

———

Pierce the armour of thought,
unlock the stillness beyond,
relinquish the fear.

———

When the language flips,
you descend into gossip,
then you have lost it.

———

If you get rebuked
and appear to have lost it, hold back,
don't fight back.

———

Fear breeds in darkness,
loses meaning in stillness,
fades out in the light.

———

Haiku

Watch the burning sky
You close your eyes for me
As you fly away in